Landscaping For Beginners

The Ultimate Guide to Create the Perfect Garden Design

By

Roger French

—

Table of Contents

Introduction

Have you ever been sitting — only sitting — in your backyard, wondering, wandering about, and soaking in the view? Never aiming directly at something, just talking of everything and anything to do with your backyard, telling yourself, "What if I placed a tree there?" And, "what will I bring in their place if I transfer those bricks?" It is, in a sense, irrelevant whether you were conscious of this or not because what you have done is to visually make this patch of property your own and come up with concepts and opinions to enhance your outer space.

And, everything in your current neighborhood and community appears to have unused, manicured grass and beautiful landscapes full of texture and color. You want an equally lovely yard, but there is no cash available in your spending plan for a landscape architect and a professional design after you buy your house. All right, so you cannot invest the capital, but can you spend the time to do it of your own? If your answer to that is yes, you might just be able to develop your own luscious, inspiring garden.

Welcome to the field of landscape architecture then — whether it is for the first or tenth time. The idea of garden architecture is nothing new: man delineated available space to its full benefit when Man initially cultivated land and concealed his agricultural land crops and livestock. This may not be architecture as we now consider it (then, naturally, esthetics were of little functional value), but he was constructing need-based spatial relations. He built his atmosphere to match the regular, weekly, seasonal, and yearly needs of his person. After then, the method of creating a landscape has changed according to design, fashion, talent, ability, aptitude, wealth, travel, creativity, and tradition, yet it can all be boiled down to the first need. Essentially, gardening is more about a person having a degree of influence over his or her climate. In addition, indeed, today is all landscape architecture. The fact is that certain methods in landscaping are so simple that you can apply them to your own garden. You just need to get an idea of these core tenets and be prepared to put the effort and time into it. There is an equally demanding intellectual and artistic challenge, above the hard physical work of landscaping your own lawn.

In order to create an aesthetically appealing landscape design, you must first see exactly what you want to create. A well-thought-out layout is the result of rational preparation and plant life, expense, and maintenance considerations.

Chapter 1: The Difference a Landscape Makes

By nature, to be clearly considered as "landscaping" a land, on the grounds of that property, you must make changes (or preserve past changes)-either in a functional or an artistic way. To an expanded context, anything that exists outside of the house on the properties is part of the landscaping of property itself. A similar term is "landscape." You indulge in landscaping while you're landscaping your yard.

In plain words, if you can see a specified feature in your lawn that affects your residence's broader aesthetic appeal or realistic functioning, then that characteristic is part of the estate's "landscaping." It can also be remembered that certain of the functional aspects of one's landscaping, such as deep irrigation networks, are important even if they remain unnoticed.

1.1 Understanding the concept of Landscaping

Landscaping is a discipline oriented to the task of planning, implementing, and preserving the surrounding land of a house. This covers aspects of furniture, landscape, and architectural design but is not restricted to. A successful landscaper demonstrates ingenuity in his work by transforming a natural area into a special, usable setting that suits the homeowners' tastes. It necessitates a basic understanding of intricate designs and botany in that particular location, under weather and terrain limitations and reimbursements.

Landscaping may be a daunting attempt to dive into it for purposes of economical and dedication. However, if you find yourself on this list, the first phase to the landscaping project has already been completed: performing your homework, which is the research, and this book will help you to do so.

You require particular abilities to do landscaping for a profit. It depends on how far you are planning to expand your business. Some landscaping experts only do side tasks related to sustaining the looks of backyards, while others can generate something special and unique. Through using stone blocks, fountains as well as other objects that create a very distinctive look, they will be capable of transforming the landscape from front or back location. If you choose to start your own company or just get landscaping work, these are the qualities you will need to perform well in this industry.

What Skill Sets Are Required for Landscaping

Landscaping will most of the time, require three particular skills. Firstly, you need to understand precisely how to construct different landscape elements. That might be plants, trees, rocks, as well as other inert yet human-made products like gazebos, seating areas, and tables. The second goal you need to have out is the capacity to do hard work. It can be extremely labor-intensive. You may need to dig or lift heavy objects, all of which will necessitate that a person is in shape. Eventually, if you are trying to integrate for a landscaping career, you must be accurate in terms of the hours you can work.

How Long Would It Take For This Type Of Role To Train?

If you are training for this type of role, you may need a few weeks to acclimatize to the whole procedure. A few of these services will make starting with their curriculum easy for you. Practice programs are common to many industries, but with landscaping, on-the-job training is simply called. As soon as you can get in and continue for a couple of years with this sort of company, it might be sufficient to start your own business.

What Degree Form Can You Use?

Despite not needing a degree, you may also want to suggest studying for a degree in anything similar to home or architecture. Identifying the essentials of how items relate to each other, whether on the inside or outdoors, can assist this form of the industry really. A landscaper is not just someone supplying repairs. They are hired from ideas they have and those offered by their clients to develop a magical scenery. An integral part of this industry is this understanding of spatial concepts.

The landscaping economy wants a few other skills. However, if you want to move into this business, it is nice to have a grasp of spatial principles and colors. It helps you create a lovely scene close to drawing before utilizing any physical artifacts. As you become more skilled in this, you will be able to complete everything much faster. It is a wonderful way to earn a living, and if you are thinking of following a business model, you might want to consider opening your own landscaping business.

Landscaper Concerns for Interview

For landscapers, landscape technicians, and landscape architects, here is a list of commonly asked questions for interviews. If you come ready to discuss examples that illustrate your skill sets, you are sure to please if you are able to share a portfolio of pictures of your past work, better still.

- What forms of landscaping projects have you been working on in the past?
- How much instruction do you enjoy getting on a task?
- Will you want single or community work? Why? For what?
- What is your organized or built landscape favorite? Why?
- What was your project with the most success? Why do you think that was successful?

- List two primary solutions to the mud.

- How many types of insect killers do you prefer to use?

- Tell us about a venture you have been working with other landscapers on that implicated collaboration.

- How would you react if you were asked by a customer to make a modification to which you did not comply?

- Until choosing plants to be produced, what soil factors should be considered?

- What do you think about organic crop production?

- Inform us of an occasion when you have successfully addressed a difficult plant disease.

- Describe a time when your layout has not turned out as anticipated. What measures have you taken to address the problem?

- What is your background in producing an advertising item or product concept?

- Do you have some experience building a design model using AutoCAD? If so, how did you apply AutoCAD to your landscaping operations?

1.2 The Importance of Landscaping

Landscapes and enhancements are essential because they contribute meaningfully to our health and quality of life. They provide the greater picture we are living our lives in. Our perception of wellness is enhanced by living within visually appealing and culturally meaningful landforms. Visiting largely unexplored scenery allows people to stay connected with the natural environment and recharge their brains and bodies.

Landscapes play a significant role in the economy is actively funding the tourism and movie industries and improving the 'green and clean' image of any country by providing value to the export markets. High-quality ecosystems can boost local communities by drawing locals and developing in an environment and visitors alike. Agricultural ecosystems promote a variety of critical practices such as cultivation, woodland, and botany.

For various purposes, individuals appreciate specific ecosystems. Some landscapes are valued for their high natural aesthetics.

These include globally renowned ecosystems such as Milford Sounds, Wakatipu Bay, the Southern Alps, the Central Volcanic Plateau, and wild and mostly undeveloped coastal regions, forests, mountains, streams, and rivers. Many ecosystems are admired for their distinctive or exceptional character that emerged over time from the interplay of nature and human forces. Such landscapes might become an integral part of local community identity. They provide a keen sense for inhabitants and frequent visitors the same as each other to relate to 'our place.' Finding a well-paved yard enhances all of the property's design aesthetic. From lighting systems to rose bushes, top-notch lawn maintenance, and water systems, you will take advantage of better landscaping. Here are primary reasons why landscaping matters:

Prevents Your Land From Deterioration

Erosion is a hazard to every yard. The soil can deviate significantly from the plant species and flower gardens as rain and wind transition along with all your assets. Stones can become demolished in steep places, presenting a risk to the safety of your children. A good landscaping design plan would work with shear structures to help stop deterioration, especially in steep areas.

These building materials could be both alluring and operational, helping to keep the soil where it originally belonged. while also supplying the plants and carvings with a lovely structure.

Break Larger Areas into Nooks

When you have a vast estate, creating private places where your neighbors likely will not see in can be hard. Landscape architecture enables even a full yard to separate into isolated and welcoming areas.

The proper design can create an outdoor living space constructed by shrubs and trees to prevent the town's noise and build a sense of being out in natural surroundings. The layout will consider how you manage to use the storage and make the best setting and theme for your needs. Your creativity only limits the options.

Prevents Your Yard From Flooding

Without a stable landscaping strategy, whenever the storm comes in the spring and fall, your lawn could turn into a mud puddle.

If you are yard downpours, the seedlings and original land development in your yard can be damaged, while making the area inaccessible. The correct design will prompt rainwater and runoff into an assigned drainage basin while redirecting the water from your plant species.

Adds Worth

Appropriate landscaping creates a cost to a residence. Landscape and bright lights can be the difference between selling your home, and not attempting to sell it. Skilled landscaping is anticipated to raise the price of your asset from 10 to 12 percent. If you are considering giving away your home, an inadequately landscaped yard can drastically decrease your property's value.

Curb Call

A well-paved yard makes the residence look as composed like a man in a custom-made suit. However, this is not just about the potted plants: it is also about the shrubbery, trees, and accents. Also, do not downplay your lawn situation. If you give the plant beds and accents all your interest but disregard the lawn, it is still not going to make a difference. The cleaner and more abundant the yard looks, the happier you can act, and the neighbors. You could even encourage your peers to landscape their yards too.

Resource Efficient

You may not recognize that, but professional landscaping can help with your home's energy-efficiency. Skilled landscaping should prepare for shade trees, help your residence stay fresher, and prevent you from operating your air conditioning unit as hard as possible. Windbreaks can be provided by a properly landscaped yard, which significantly reduces the heating costs. Landscaping can also assist in storm water control, enabling adequate runoff after heavy rainfall or snow melts to avoid flooding.

Serenity

A beautifully landscaped yard would offer you a beautiful, attractive spot to settle down and rest or invite the company to enjoy. That is why it is worth bringing the work into your yard, alone. There are many explanations for the value of landscaping; these are only a handful. A specialist should have expertise in fields such as; when flowers bloom and how large they get, what healthy soil is, how to make your lawn grow green and lush, where to put a walkway that does not harm the flow of storm water, and how to grade your flowerbeds and yard to prevent floods.

Creates Natural Habitats

Landscape plans should not always be increased-maintenance. Many methods use native plants and vegetation to make a stunning ecosystem that thrives season after season. If a design incorporates plants that are local to the tropical, the landscaping would be well suited to accommodate the regular weather shifts without your or the landscaping team needing particular time and consideration. Soil, natural weather, and temperature fluctuations may all present a threat to non-native plants. Still, Network-born varieties get all the resources they want from the regional topsoil without extra artificial fertilizer.

On top of this, as the architecture imitates the natural world, insects, squirrels, and other tiny requirements are encouraged to create a home there.

Treat Your Landscape as a Separate Ecosystem

By the start of a great and intense day, the backyard is more than just a spot to disengage; it is an environmentalist-system in and of itself. The Land's shifting slope shaded zones, and sunshine places have specific requirements to be determined before they can be utilized. A good landscape design considers these considerations and views the yard like an ecosystem, putting the best plants in the right location. The outcome is a layout that plans sewage, erosion, and plant-life sustainability.

Reduces Environmental Impact

You can attach plants and flowers that are not well adapted to the New York conditions while you are growing a flowerbed yourself. You can need to apply nitrogen to the soil to mitigate the impact of the environmental patterns, soil composition, and humidity.

Most commonly produced fertilizers are made of environmentally damaging chemicals; although they help, your tropical flowers thrive in the summer months.
When the rain comes, the fertilizer left in the soil enters the water source, which poses a danger to the natural fauna and native plants.

Landscape architecture requires consideration of biodiversity for each scheme. Although those favorite native plants may be used in one design area, they are not going to be needed in every area. Restricting the usage of exotic or non-native plants reduces the environmental impact of the landscaping.

Although improving the curb appeal or resale value of your home is a bonus of successful landscape design, the real advantage is your landscaping quality, how your yard is converted, and the satisfaction you get from spending quality time in the yard.

Regulatory privileges of Landscapes

- Natural Coolants - Grass is much colder than pavement or concrete. This serves as an environmentally safe "climate conditioner." Typically, lawns will be 31 degrees fresher than pavement and 20 degrees fresher than bare earth. Yet wait, there is more to it. Homes shielding by trees will lower overhead temperatures by something like 40 degrees.

- Natural cleaners of the environment - Grass perform a crucial function of trapping pollen, particulate matter from smoking, and other contaminants and generate oxygen.

- Water Protectors - Safe lawns will trap polluted pollution that may potentially flow into water bodies.

- Air purifiers – Grasses consume and decompose co2 into oxygen and fuel. A 50'x50 "lawn actually produces sufficient oxygen for a family of three.

- Disturbance Minimizers – shrubs and plants significantly reduce noise pollution; over hard floors such as asphalt and pavement, they can reduce the emissions by 20 to 30 percent. Turf grass rates down and removes discharges into water sources. It is critical that lawns and ecosystems remain a niche component of healthy cities, even in areas that have water shortages and are experiencing drought. There is a range of sustainability solutions that will enable the reduction of water use by controlled lawns and ecosystems but still provide significant environmental benefits.

Privileges of Urban Landscapes

A rising body of work is revealing how necessary it is to integrate tree canopies and gardens into towns and cities.

They deliver a wide variety of lifestyle advantages that enhance the residents' standard of living. Parks and canopies in forest areas tend to minimize noise.

A new, U.S. research Forest Service finds that tree-lined streets and bigger yard trees had common crime levels in neighborhoods. Research suggests that staring at the plants and trees will minimize tension and lower blood even through a glass. As per a study by Marc Rosenberg of the University of Chicago, walking in a natural setting of plants and trees, even though situated in the center of an area, has been shown to boost focus and memory. Neighborhoods who integrate open fields in the neighborhood report reduced depression incidences decreased health insurance rates, and increased quality of life.

Urban Landscapes Profits

Businesses are most effective in offering landscaped areas outside buildings and plants within structures to their consumers.

Research showed that occupancy prices for industrial offices with better quality environments were seven percent higher. Shoppers continue to pay nine to 12 percent more on services and products in city centers that have tarps of a high-quality forest. Shoppers say they are likely to drive a larger distance and longer to reach an area with a high-quality forest canopy, and then invest some time there until they get there.

Companies that provide experiences with nature to their workers often profit. Rachael Kaplan, Ph.D., undertook studies found that there was a significantly higher career and life satisfaction and improved wellbeing in employees who could observe nature from their desks.

Psychological and Physical Gains

Equally well understood and recorded are the effects of human contact with plants, trees, and grass. Evidence also has shown that when people communicate with nature or simply experience it from a lens, they feel emotional reduction and healing. Since going outside, adolescents with ADHD tend to be concentrating more (Harvard Health Publications). Employees are often more efficient while dealing with plants in settings, which enhances executive performance.

Yet, even more, important than what research teaches us is what people naturally believe in their minds regarding the plants and green spaces — that the connection makes their life happier, and they want to make an attempt to integrate it into their minds.

Data from the 2012 Husqvarna Global Garden Report found that "63 percent of respondents indicated a willingness to pay extra for a house or property if it is situated in an environment with good green spaces, contrasted, for example, with 34 percent willing to pay more for a good retail environment and 33 percent willing to pay for good cultural sites."

1.3 Differentiating between Landscaping and Gardening

Certain individuals often get confused with landscapers and gardeners. Perhaps they cannot really tell the gap between the two to be more accurate. It is a gray area, so let us clarify some common misunderstandings.

If you are landscaping or planting, all entail designing practical, esthetically appealing outdoor environments, and preserving them. Both practices may be interests or professions in tiny backyards or beaches, golf resorts, and construction buildings. While gardening and landscaping are identical, distinctions exist within them.

16th-century Dutch artists used the term "landschap" to characterize land-based depictions of the landscape.

The current English term "landscape" collects from the Netherlands and relates to a mental representation of spaces outside.

Therefore, landscaping is about envisioning an image for a room and then constructing it. Landscaping combines botanical elements such as plants, lawns and trees and bushes and other vegetation, along with hardscapes such as paths, benches, beds for planting, ponds, and fences, into the area.

Landscape Experts

Landscape professionals, builders, and builders provide activities that are different but intersect. Landscape architects need a qualification in a built environment, and to receive a license, they must undergo a regional test. These practitioners operate on a range of styles and sizes of initiatives, from the design and construction of a residential yard to the designing of transport infrastructure, parks, and waterfront projects Landscape architects do not need advanced qualifications, although technical bodies based on their history of design practice may certify them.

 Designers usually focus on small-scale or private designs, so after finishing the design process, they cannot generally deal with landscape contractors. Landscape contractors execute the artist or designer's dream by designing the buildings and adding the botanic and hardscape components. Contractors may even restrict their company to yard and garden repairs, in which situation they are simply gardeners.

Gardening

Gardening entails design, planning, and servicing, as does landscaping, but gardening typically requires only the seedlings in a space. Landscape planners and gardeners may draw a garden concept and decide a planting list, but the plants can only be grown, weeded, tended, rotated, and harvested. Gardening is a continuous process, as gardens require year-round tending and skilled care. Gardening often includes awareness of different natural systems, including soil biology, environments, plant morphology, water runoff, and infestations of pests, through practice and research.

Professionals in Gardening

Skilled gardeners could be graduating in botany or horticulture. Other qualified gardeners may have a master gardener curriculum completed. In general, master gardener systems involve several weeks of practice from professional and academic mentors in the field of horticulture or gardening. The Master Gardeners of the California system, for example, needs more than 50 hours of training coupled with regular service hours and continuing education quotas.

Garden Range

Gardens may differ from basic flower to stone gardens layout. Gardening may be particular to a combination of plants for a specific form of plant or fruit or tree. Next to home are home plants; rain gardens that grow water plants or crops around lakes; rock gardens use the height produced by rocks to position plants in or around the rocks. Many homeowners plan rock gardens in their yards to target rugged slopes. Some bring rocks onto clean, reckless yards. With planting, the garden environment is only mildly altered. Pretty much the entire plots may be mined by heavy equipment in landscaping, and the landscape may be modified by planting not only plants but also various varieties of the soil environment that may not be native to the region. Landscapers often refer to gardeners as 'plantsmen' since a gardener insists on plant protection and well-being. Landscapers are usually active as driveways, patios, walls, and related jobs regarded as 'hardscaping.' A significant distinction between a gardener and a landscaper is the degree to which they are eligible for the job. Landscapers typically need one or two different commercial licenses. We may require a construction authorization to create a gazebo or pool or require paving or concreting permission to do 'hardscaping' work.

Landscapers would need to use heavy machinery, too. Having said that, several business associations or bigger businesses may have the expertise and resources to provide planting and landscaping facilities.

Therefore, Who Should I Hire, A Landscaper, Or A Gardener?

When you search in a horticultural perspective to get your garden restored or brought back to life, and emphasis on plant growth, a gardener is a way to go. If you want your garden to be fully renovated or revamped or want a significant new addition to be added, all you need is a landscaping specialist or maybe a skilled landscape planner to plan and a landscaper to do the installation.

Similitudes

- Both ought to have the freedom to arrange plants and other features to build a garden they love.
- All gardeners and landscapers should have some horticulture information, like plant life expectancies and growing plants; perform better than others in certain conditions.
- A gardener would undoubtedly be delighted to deliver some 'softscaping' such as restoring walls, adding decorative gravel, and mulch.

- **Competencies Needed For Gardening**
- Recognize pests in the garden and of plant species
- Lopping the Vine
- Arbitrary pruning
- Expertise in native plants
- Understanding of the services of the garden such as the aeration of the lawn and the abolishment of thatch.

Chapter 2: Different Landscape Designs

In terms of architecture, style applies to the way we convey ideas and arrange fabrics, plants, materials, and decorations in order to build a structure that is recognizable and appreciable. While some landscape styles are short-lived trends, some are inspirational, each with its own purposes and motifs. Enforced visual and spatial rhythm is maintained using the classically inspired structured form, order, improvisation, and axial uniformity.

In comparison, Modernism, which established in the early 20th century as a prominent trend in landscape and garden design, utilizes asymmetry to develop complex views across the area, and several designers today have adopted aspects of this style to attain sleek, clean gardens. Others followed a more flexible strategy, establishing their own collection of guidelines, and discovering innovative methods of producing harmonious structures. Landscape designs typically take influence from cultural or historical points of reference, which offer them a common theme. The goal is to establish a stylized depiction of truth rather than a detailed portrayal of fact. For, e.g., Japanese-style gardens sometimes neglect the original metaphysical and religious sense but are atmospheric nevertheless.

The typical cottage garden is likewise a strongly romanticized image of the simplified artisan style. Broader problems and changes in lifestyles also helped shape the site in order. The influx of foreign travel has provided gardeners a glimpse of al fresco life (as can be seen in areas such as the Mediterranean) and more tropical planting, which is progressively being used in urban landscapes where sunny microclimates enable a wider range of plants to flourish. Meanwhile, environmental issues motivate the usage of recycled resources and wildlife planting.

2.1 Types of Landscape Designs

The finest landscape layouts are indeed the ones meticulously planned out with an eye for detail. It is crucial to assess what design will best suit your residence and way of living before designing a landscape.

Continuing to work for how much you have is among the most valuable aspects of landscape architecture. E.g., if you are looking for a formal English garden, but your yard requirements do not match it, it will never turn outright. However, you should try to incorporate drought-resistant crops and dry elements into your landscape architecture if you reside in an arid region.

There are a couple of factors you can consider when deciding a landscape or lawn style:

- What sort of environments are there in your yard? Is the place mostly cloudy or very warm?
- Which style of scenery better fits your style of life?
- Would you need a low-maintenance garden, or do you enjoy taking care of your yard most of the time?
- Which style of a landscape would best enhance your residence?
- Which type of activities are you going to use your yard for?

Who is going to use the yard? Would you consider having kids or pets?

There are various significant styles of landscaping and gardening, which you can then prototype your own. Alternatively, you can be inventive, incorporating elements from multiple methods to generate your design look.

English-style Landscape

The English Garden Design makes use of several shrubs and perennials in a scheme complementing your home's underlying theme. Other elements of decoration could include an arbor or a birdbath.

Oriental Countryside

Using a range of plants, the Oriental Style utilizes soil, bricks, and greenness to create unique viewpoints. You might even suggest incorporating a typical Zen Japanese garden.

Woodland Countryside.

The Woodland Design represents the natural way fauna develops in a wooded environment with a less manicured look than certain other landscape types. When you do not want to waste a lot of money on upkeep that will be a smart option.

Formal Countryside

Of order, well-pruned crops, the Formal Style exhibits symmetrical patterns, clear lines, and complex geometrical elements. These landscapes often feature topiary design. This aesthetic of landscaping requires considerable maintenance.

Informally Designed Landscape

The Informal Design utilizes edging plant beds that are curved. Plants are organized according to unrelated designs. If you have boys running in the neighborhood, this will be a smart idea.

Gardens of Butterflies

Dozens of the butterfly or species of birds that are native to your region make particular gardens a welcoming addition. Many plant species have a supply of calories and are useful to draw such flying mates. Creating free and wind safe areas.

The Jardine of Xeriscape

The yard or greenhouse consumes as many as 50 percent of household energy. This practice for habitats involves plenty of low-water trees and plants and developing strategies to minimize moisture absorption.

Garden of the Mediterranean

This type of garden is wide walls lined with abundant olive groves, conifers, or cypress plants. Sometimes, a water feature or flowing water pond is needed. Splayed rosemary or other surface coverings that spill out of the walls or into big bags. Lilacs are working well along or around buildings, as structured hedges. Plants that bloom a green, gray, or purple spikey flower can provide to this garden theme. Bougainvillea mounted around walls with light color.

Garden Cottage

This type is called a garden of old age. Try including the lilac, hydrangea, plum, and mauve plants. The perennials that we have listed will fit well with this style. Herbs are also wonderful in a Cottage garden - rosemary, sweet bay, cranberries, and figs fit this garden-style perfectly. A neatly trimmed lawn with floating flowers at the bottom. It is a landscape with substantial upkeep, plenty of soil, and constant pruning and fertilization.

Bio Farms

As even more individuals learn the negative impacts of many toxic substances, naturally growing plants are becoming more prevalent. This implies the use of natural forms of insect management and implantation, rather than artificial fertilizers or sprays.

Consider if you have a landscape scenery you are pleased with, you will be spending considerably more time in your lawn. In addition, if you have a yard that you can frequently use, it is like having space in your house.

Chapter 3: Steps to Get Started for Beginners

Finding solutions is all that designing your landscape is about. At first, it can sound daunting, but if you begin with a clear idea of your goals and practical needs, your basic design will quickly start to take shape. Start by drawing all your inspirations together, using magazines, photographs, and online sources to create a book or ideas folder. Your images might include plants and landscapes that you love, and maybe furniture or art that you admire. You should also create a basic bubble diagram to better explain your feelings and describes places for multiple tasks, such as eating and drinking, sleeping, or playing room for the baby. The routes of paths, structural shapes, and spaces between elements all have an impact on a design's look and feel, and need to be considered before you draw up a finished plan. For instance, sinuous paths and organic forms combine to create relaxed and informal designs, while straight paths and symmetric layouts convey a formal look. - the location will have its own specific challenges, whether your garden is on a steep slope and requires terracing, or whether it is a small or uncomfortable shape.

Whatever the issue, it would help to learn how to use curves, forms, height, form, and viewpoints. You may also use a number of strategies to direct or mislead the eye, build an impression of room in a tiny area, or redirect attention to reflect on particular characteristics. The colors, patterns, and textures that you choose have a strong impact when it comes to creating atmosphere and moods. The impression of size and space in the garden is also affected by the color — cool blues and whites tend to make an area look larger; warm reds and yellows create spaces appear lively and compact. Pale, white colors reflect light into dull plots. Texture can also be used to great effect by mixing rough with smooth, or polished with matte to create exciting contrasts. In the field of landscape design, there are no rights or wrongs, so have fun and play.

3.1 Fundamental Principles of a Landscape Design

The design standards are rules and can be used to help transfer the broad generalizations of landscaping concepts to details. This requires seven characteristics, which would cause every layout to be coherent, seamless, and beautiful when provided proper regard. Often, these ideas can influence how the design looks, moves, and works. There is no clear structure or order of these concepts. Based on the case, they can be important may not relevant at all. These are common concepts, which are easy to recognize. When recognized and incorporated, their effect would greatly enhance any ecological nature of the landscape.

The Seven Gestural Concepts of Designing a Landscape: Plainness

It is necessary to remove elements that do not include enhancement or effect on architecture. In order to maintain the environment tidy, orderly and uncluttered, consider what is essential and what is not so. A basic, excellently defined template is one that will make the software easy to manage and develop.

Options

Selections in color, scale, and style will be varied for generating visual appeal. Should not sacrifice convenience, though, solely to build varied variations.

Balance

Anything that is put in a design must bring with it a specific visual weight. Balance is the idea of meaning that sometimes the entire program has weight. A strategy of formal equilibrium would see all sides mimicking each other, whereas informal equilibrium corresponds to similar but not identical. Both can function well.

Importance

Emphasizing areas of the design utilizing form, shape, or color will create attention and guide the eye via the design, but too much focus may seem messy. Areas of organisms are better left alone. Accent places are intended to stand out even within a broader architectural sense. Core plants may help to relax or de-emphasize design forms.

Order

The sequence refers to how shifts are applied in the aspects of plant size, shape as well as texture. Gradual modifications of one component at a time give a smooth, enticing series — abrupt shifts from a tall plant to a small, or a good-textured plant to a rugged one.

Scale / Size

The size of the elements in a landscape is proportion and is relative to how they respond to each other. It will all match the scale of the landscape and the things in it. A fence or tree that is far bigger than the majority of the landscape can draw the attention away from all else.

Harmony

Harmony is the idea that it all fits well. Interconnection is creating cohesion by utilizing links to dynamically link places such as roads, sidewalks, steps, and fences.

Repetition happens as a concept feature unifies, as it exists in many environments. Repeat may be beneficial, so be cautious not to overburden it. Dominance occurs where one common focal point, like a big tree, tends to unify certain places of support.

3.2 Choosing the Ideal Landscape Design

If your yard wants only fresh seedlings or a full refreshment, it can be daunting to overhaul the garden. For the ideal garden, here are a few should-know landscape architecture ideas.

If you have never before attempted an outdoor space design, all of the options you may make can surprise you. However, if you speak about it within your home as space, it makes things even simpler. The same concepts, which guide the setup of your room inside, should also direct your designs outdoors. You are capable of managing a room together – so your scenery should not be a problem! Here are a few concepts for starters of landscape architecture.

Evaluate the Desires and Needs of the Landscape

Develop a "requires and wants" chart. Do your children require room to play? Want to raise vegetables? Would the family like to be assembled in a patio? Also, do some messy yard sketches with thoughts where you would like to put things in; it is a wonderful ideological basis for beginner landscape architecture.

Begin Small

Home and garden TV shows are experts at showing full outdoor makeovers in only three days — but they have a 60-member crew, which is not a condition most inexperienced gardeners love. Way to create a landscape is working on a plan slowly and enjoying the challenge. Focus on a small flowerbed, from your grand plan. When you have the time, go out there and collaborate on it for two hours, and worry that much about clogging everything up immediately.

Write About Where to Go

Research the movements of Sun and Air. You may decide to put a deck on the south side of the building, but it will get loads of afternoon heat, which means September's dinnertime will not be soothing — just dry. So a fire pit can soon be engulfed by wind bellowing across a corner. These are all common errors for beginners of landscape design. Whatever the wind and sun do at varying periods of the day and month should be taken into account in your design.

Hold Back And Admire The Landscape.

Live time with it. Getting to fast decisions regarding your yard will contribute to long-term decisions that do not function. Within a week of spending a lot of time outside, you are going to start seeing regions where you can go and take a seat that you did not even think about at first.

Emphasis on Size and Motion

It is the hardest principle for beginners in landscape design, but magnitude and pacing give a lifted-together look to your yard. Variations of scale, form, and color may arise, with tall plants against a house or at the rear of a flowerbed, and pathways taking pedestrians across space.

 Panovich stresses the importance of striking the right balance among reiteration and unique themes. Persistence gives a sense of coherence, but you do not want it to be boring and repetitive, either. A seasonal new option is a better option than having all the various elements at all. Every effective garden plan has a central focus or set of focal points, so it is a simple concept for beginners to apply in landscape design. That could be a sculpture or a beautiful flower, a shrub, or a trilogy of trees. Let the design roll your eyes across the countryside.

Be Accessible To Modifications.

Unless you are dedicated to something, be truthful about whatever you want and like — and what might fall out of your favor. Patience is required for beginner landscaping. If all that empty space is just too much to look at, as well as the kids and animals track in dirt, rely on alternative fixes — annuals, ground cover, fast-growing surface coverings — to cover the ground while you are having figured out whatever you want.

3.3 Gathering Your Tools

In caring for our houses, you would definitely require different landscaping devices from time to time that will help the job move quicker and better. There are a variety of landscaping tools available, so let us spend the effort to obtain a deeper understanding of the most prominent options you would probably be using in divergent landscaping tasks. Were you able to make some improvements to your lawn? Would you want to do all of it yourself? You will need a bunch of options first. We have created a list of our top important landscaping and gardening resources, which you will need before launching your next growing project.

Landscaping Edger

This is a versatile product you will use to clean the garden's edges. Say, if you have overgrown some of your grasses or plants and already cover certain sections of your paths or curbs, you can use the edger to remove them.

Edgers Types

- Electronic – At one point, battery-driven machines were unreliable. In contrast, today's electronic devices are, by far, the safest way to go. In some situations, you might need to spend a little bit more on finding the best tool, but items like tune-ups, persnickety tools, etc. are a distant memory! This method is perfect to use for lawn cutting and flowering.
- Fuel-powered – it is a wireless edger that provides a huge benefit because you do not have to think about wires that sockets. Therefore, you can use it even at the farthest reaches of your yard.

Maneuvers

Landscaping handcuffs if you do not want to turn green on those thumbs, you had better keep them safe. Your first level of protection against thorn bushes, nettles, splinters, soil, and diseases are suitable gardening gloves.

In addition to wearing a proper glove, you will want to consider gardening gloves, which are:

- Designed to safeguard vulnerable wrist pieces
- Water and soil prone, but breathable;
- Lasting but pleasant, easy to use and easy to use

Applications: horticulture, gardening, landscaping, construction, gardening.

Sleeves for Rinsing

For new landscapes, certain essential things are sometimes ignored. Hoses and irrigation distribute water reliably throughout your yard. Water always provides the plants with much-required nutrients and oxygen by way of their stems. Look for a suitable irrigation device or hose with:

- Rubber construction so as not to kink and tangle
- Bottom line length for correct pressure amount
- Parts or nozzles flexible to enter all areas of your landscape

Applications: drainage, planting grass, landscaping, gardening.

Fork in the Yard

When you are acquainted with Melbourne's unique soil quality, you may be mindful that certain places may be rugged and full of clay. Whether that sounds like your yard, you will need a sturdy planting fork to break up the dirt. Hold an eye out for the perfect fork:

- Is well structured and ergonomic, permitting constant usage
- Have bent tines, yet solid tines to dig and process mulch and soil

- Has clear square tines to allow inroads into solid, rough land

Applications: planting, landscaping, spreading of grass, surface enhancement, seeding

Pikes

Let us give them a spade. Because of their wide variety of uses and flexibility, spades of varying sizes and shapes are among the most valuable resources in any field. Tell someone who has attempted to dig a pit by hand or a trench. Look out for spades, which are:

- Features ergonomically crafted hardwood handles that easily absorb and disperse shock
- Feature an inexorable steel head resistant to bending and rust
- Are adequately dense and strong to break through the roots and soil while digging

Applications: mining, horticulture, landscape design, building, planting.

Tensioners

Pruning is a critical move toward planning the plants for various seasons of development. Pruning promotes strong, stable stem growth, and eliminates the infected and harmed components.

- A set of secateurs of high quality can make pruning simple, particularly if:
- Should function for several years of regular use with interchangeable blades
- Hand contour, allowing for easier use and leverage
- Its multiple features include safety locks as well as sap grooves.

Applications: to garden, to prune.

A Sharp Knife
You just have to skip to the track occasionally. Do not relegate a decent knife to the kitchen cabinet. Knives are used widely in the field, including fast cuttings, chopping string, and tiny round holes. Seek to locate a knife in the garden to:

- Is built of premium stainless steel and is rustproof
- Can be stepped up without undue effort
- Is conveniently collapsible for fast handling and protection

Applications: gardening, pruning, construction, landscape planning.

Hoes in the Yard

Garden hoes for a more rapid break-up of the field. We use a right-angled blade to reach deep into the soil, requiring limited effort to displace material. Hoes are not identical, so you are going to want to find a decent one, which is:

- Medium task, and built for the penetration of rough terrain
- Large and easy to handle, leaving your leg and backs under pressure
- Encased to stay wart-free throughout its existence

Uses: planting, field planning, digging.

Knee Protector

Lasting garden designs involves spending a great deal of time on your hands. Whether you do marijuana or drink, you will want to cover your precious joints. Knee safety is an excellent measure of prevention, enabling you to spend much more time in your yard. Find padding on knees:

- Only suit the legs necessary to avoid slipping.
- Am well developed, sponsored and padded
- Is easy to clean by machine

Uses: designed to weed, harvesting, and planting.

Garden Cart or Wheelbarrow

Make the lifting bulky and more comfortable to carry on yourself. For more extensive gardens, a wheelbarrow or cart is an integral piece of machinery that lets gardeners move dirt, gravel, trees, leave, or other content throughout the garden. You are going to like a wheelbarrow or a garden cart, which is:

- Well perfectly shaped and well equilibrated
- Practical, robust, and rustproof
- Graciously contoured, with capacities reaching 100L

Applications: construction, landscaping, horticulture.

A Multifunction Ratchet

When you consider a landscape device that crosses a number of buttons, you can go there. Multifunctional rakes may catch leaves and waste, scoop some items, and sift dirt. You will want a multipurpose rake, as a young aspiring gardener:

- Can take the form of several unfavorable instruments at once
- Is made of light but heavy content such as polycarbonate
- Can shoot holes to ventilate the soil

3.4 Step by Step Detailed Guide to the Process of Landscaping

A landscape design is like an outdoor recreational floor plan. A landscape design provides a dramatic portrayal of a site utilizing scaled components, just like a floor layout. Landscape designs contain natural features such as roses, plants, and fields, as well as fabricated things such as garden furniture, pavilions, and shelters. Landscape projects can provide drainage and brightness overlays, too.

Landscape designs are mainly used for planning the design for an open environment, whether that is a private garden plan for your residence or a business or public plan. They are also helpful when truly innovative installation or restoration is required or when making plans for an outdoor event. The creation of a landscape plan can also help with material selection in the process of decision-making. It also offers improved metrics for a cost analysis for the property owner and the landscape designer, helping to ensure that the job will be done under financial constraints.

How to Construct a Landscape Design

Build a contour. A landscape design begins with a detailed outline of the project area. That is your general overview, to which you may incorporate elements gradually. Decide what region to include in the figure. This may be challenging because of the distributed nature of an outside environment, but the built environment should only demonstrate the region that is subject to the landscaping. Start by drawing zone boundaries. It may be the side of a lawn, the lawn end, a barrier, or some other place in which the landscape design is no longer relevant. Connect functions already in operation. Introduce any stones, water bodies, tower blocks, railings, slopes, etc. during the landscaping procedure that cannot or will not be relocated. For these, too, make sure to use the right icons and colors. Essentially these help in the area's creativity when completed. You may want to mention the South on your map to help you appreciate how the scenery will be altered by the sunlight and reflections. If required, build ground cover. Fill out the field with the correct form of ground cover styles (such as lawn of asphalt) to be built. For a more realistic representation of such regions, add textures.

Connect modern concepts of landscape architecture. Add vegetation such as shrubbery, bushes, and flowers and draw along walks and stairs.

Fill in any patio furniture, fountains, sheds, tree houses, buildings, and ponds you plan on building.

Landscape Maintenance

For every landscape, the very first point to mention is that it is a living, breathing being. Only the smallest, easiest-to-care yard requires the avoidance of irrigation, food, cleaning, and infection. If you are not a massive supporter of yard upkeep, it may well be smart to implement easy-to-maintain landscaping. In reality, landscape management requires far more than the typical homeowner assumes. Mowing, replanting, and weeding are sometimes performed but rarely completed correctly. The distinction between good and weak preserving the environment is always in the specifics. Taking the additional few minutes to do the best thing would pay back big rewards in the future, with a more attractive lawn and fewer maintenance problems.

So, how are you getting the job correct? Simple: You are researching, creating, and diligently following a checklist for landscape maintenance. In this helpful guide, we have done the analysis for you, but that is just a guideline for your particular lawn and landscape design. Specific landscaping and design features can involve your own maintenance products, but it will get you going.

Areas to be cultivated.

Some plant species require regular focus, whereas others will add nothing to maintaining your landscape. Test your plant's condition during summer. Covering the field with soil amendments can help maintain moisture in the soil and hold the weeds at bay. Cut back branches of plants during the first hard freeze and coat them with mulch. Most flowers perform best when they are deadheaded (i.e., pinch off the spent blooms), encouraging new growth.

Controlling bugs

Often with a good jet of water, a plant may be wiped away free. Many garden centers are marketing bugs such as ladybugs to rid themselves of bugs and worms. Toxins are an alternative, too, but, when using them, use strict care. Take into account using "natural" in-household substances for insect control. For starters, putting a submerged plate soaked in beer in your insect-infested landscape would typically draw certain pests and destroy them.

1. **Weeding**

The only effective solution is to get rid of it is to cut the whole plant by the roots. Fertilizers do operate but implement vigilance.

That way, you are going to destroy not just the herb but other surrounding plants as well. Hold weeds to a minimal by making a foot or two of mulch cover the surface.

2. Prevention of weeds

An inch-thick mulch layer will keep your planting beds comparatively free from weeds. The grass is a plant that, when healthy, grows dense and bushy and will generally suffocate out certain weeds. Any inorganic fertilizers start with a "pre-emergent" that destroys the seeds while the plants are inactive in the morning.

3. Making moves

Do not cut the grass too early while it is too short. Lengthier vegetation is safer, in addition to which it also absorbs sunlight. Most mowers come with a choice to mulch, which cuts grass into tiny pieces and adds them to the field. It contributes essential nutrients to the soil and lessens fertilizer requirements.

4. Removing leaves

Clear the leaves off grassy fields. The surface of leaves will limit the intensity of the light near the roots to the lawn and to collect water.

5. **Nutrition**

Fertilize the lawn and rising flower or grass beds three to four times per planting season, based on the climate. Offering both organic and chemical options.

6. **Hedge trim and tree trim**

Seasonal pruning is expected of trees and shrubs. Prune off old trees as well as active branches that get out of hand. In the season, several hedges ought to be post-shaped many times but rarely prune or cut during the fall. It would promote development at a period when plants are supposed to be inactive.

7. **Servicing Sprinkler**

During fall, winter your sprinkler system by draining or "blowing out" the water from the pipelines and close down the time limit. You will need to reboot the system in the spring by turning the time limit and the professional valve on.

8. **Clean up from spring**

Raising the remaining foliage and garbage that has been piling up during the winter months. Try adding a fresh mulch coat to cover the new shoots from freezing.

Mulch will operate its way into the environment over time and regenerate it. Consider mulch consisting of tiny sustainable parts such as "bark fines" or cocoa shells recycled. Mulch produced from bigger pieces of wood, such as strips of cedar or aspen, will demand a much longer time to process.

9. Thatching

Thatch is a coating of dead vegetation that accumulates somewhere above the surface of the soil over time and must be discarded. During the spring period, aerate and de-thatch whilst the grass is still inactive.

10. Core airing

At least aerate the lawn twice a year to enable air and water to flow in and outside of the soil.

3.5 Common Mistakes of Landscaping and Their Solutions

Whether you're caring for your own landscape, or someone is keeping it for you, here are some basic errors that we often see in the landscapes. Learn to stop these errors to save money, content to stress for yourself.

Realize it or not, constructing a badly planned landscape will cost as much as building a well built one. In addition, when you are forking mega-money to build your aspirations' outdoor living space or greenhouse, having the concept correct pays off. Nevertheless, more and more time you spend on the nature of the outdoor landscape by analyzing the complexities, the more acquainted you are with the product. This prevents unwanted occurrences before or after the team has vacated the yard during the building confusion.

- **Not Hiring A Landscaper Or Builder For The Works Concerned**

If you've got a big lawn or great expectations, landscaping can be a complex and difficult undertaking, and obtaining a professional landscape onboard could save you days of wasted effort and cash. A landscape expert will make optimum use of the regions you have and set priorities for grass layouts, enjoyable areas, ponds, and much more.

- **Not Improvising a Budget**

Are you aware that landscaping is 30% more costly than any other home renovation method? Setting your expenditure is wise when you are beginning a landscaping venture. If you are beginning fresh, landscaping is advised for 10 to 15 percent of your construction budget.

- **Not Planning The Layout Analytically**

Your land appears as a centralized totality, and so landscaping should not continue to function in silos, but stream from one component to the next effortlessly. In this particular regard, a good landscape developer can assist. Take a move back to look at your yard as if someone unfamiliar to your residence may think how all the landscape design for the entire image fits together.

Trees Planted In Too Much Depth

Unlike other life forms, tree species consist of various tissue types that play different roles.

Bark structure supports the plant and holds nutrition between the roots and the plants while root tissue retains soil water and nutrients. The normal horticultural procedure specifies defining and planting at or just above floor level the stage where bark tissue reaches root tissue (the root flare).

The root flare has also been hidden by dirt, either in the container or during the planting process, as plants are bought. If the step of defining the root flare is skipped during cultivating and the plant is placed too low, many bushes and nearly all trees may fail and starve in several years. In the business, we term this cellular poling because the tree appears as a telephone pole rooted in the dirt. If you glance at trees and bushes that develop naturally, you will still see the root flare, or a broadening at the foundation, as in the woods.

- **The Generated Spaces Are Too Limited For Use**

This is a common issue for tiny townhouses, apartments, or small country club homes where there is little open space, but it may also happen in broader environments. Please be careful of undersize proportions when constructing patios, sidewalks, and openings.

Not Adding Enough Irrigation

At the outset of the project, prepare the correct irrigation system, and do not make it an absolute nightmare. Each crop in your landscape design has specific watering requirements, so that should be taken into consideration by an irrigation scheme. You will also still want to cover the drainage lines since obvious irrigation really can mess up a beautiful plan.

- **Weak Clipping of the Lawn**

Although the golf course looks good, cutting the lawn like a putting green (or maybe even a fairway) is in pursuit of disaster. If the grass is too small, it absorbs more of the surface of the weed, damaging its capacity to do the photosynthetic activity. While that is bad enough, sparse vegetation also produces lackluster, undesirable roots that have nutritional absorption difficulties. Hold the turf more like the forest than like the putting green — approximately two-and-a-half to three.

- **Filling Your Lawn With Numerous Tchotchkes**

In your landscaping, there is a location for decorations but minimize intimidating your lawn with far too many tchotchkes. Ultimately, a gratuity level is defined, after which these ornaments draw attention away from your scenery, rather boosting it. A more sensible approach to utilize adornments is to do it sparingly, which would excel in drawing attention to it.

- **Scatter-Gun Harvesting**

Even when house owners pick plants that complement their setting, they still make the error of sowing one of the items they may find in the nursery. Too much variety can transform this into a hotchpotch in your landscape.

- **The appraisal of esthetics over function**

We all want a lovely backyard, but it is essential that we do not lose track of utility. Seek ways to combine features and aesthetic appeal. Sowing evergreen trees, for example, give your land color throughout the year, whilst also offering yet another coating of confidentiality. In addition, building a stone fireplace may look beautiful, but for families with young children attempting to run around everything is also not the right alternative. Ultimately, efficiency will dominate landscaping beauty, but it is feasible to provide both.

- **Disregarding exteriors**

Too many folks assume of their landscaping mostly in aspects of how it will appear throughout the day. Adding some outdoor lighting will let you display off your lawn and add a special degree of protection to your residence and your neighbors. Implementing landscape light sources need not be a big project. Adding a few solar panel lights to your lawn will give your house an enjoyable glow all evening.

Chapter 4: Preparing an Edible Yet Sustainable Landscape for Your House

Before I immerse myself in the fantastic and thrilling facets of what an edible landscape can do for you, I would like to frame up a few items. When you consider making an "edible landscape," you may believe in an entirely right scenery: where you can walk around and eat whatever you see. It is not just practically impossible, but it is also not very feasible, as marvelous, the thought of it would be. With that said, components of several food-producing plant species are by no means edible (for instance, think of rhubarb leaves), so the concept of sowing a landscape in which you can eat everything you see would be limited. Next, if you only tried to plant food crops, your landscape might end up composed of around exclusively annuals (especially for those who live in a cold climate), that doesn't do much for year-round aesthetic value and appeal or soil creation.

Third, flowering plants (annuals, perennials, shrubs, and trees) offer a lot of hue and range, retain pollinating insects and help broaden (that also seems to do an incredible role in providing pests and diseases at bay).

Of course, you might grow a whole food field environment, but by doing so, you will be losing a lot. Which is why, particularly in this book and chapter, we will talk concerning blending all sorts of different plant species: fruits, vegetables, spices, annuals, perennials, shrubs, and trees to create the most of the room you have, both aesthetically and edible.

Linking With food

Why are we landscaping or gardening? With such a free and easy permission to so much food these days, especially with farmers' harvests popping up all around the country, in several towns and cities, why should we worry about growing our food? Why should we bother landscaping or gardening? I believe one of the key reasons if either we recognize it or not is to Relate. With so much fresh produce available at all times of the year, it can be

Tough to see the link between our fruit and vegetables and the rest of the universe. No doubt, food is one of the most essential parts of our lives. Yet we let random men, hundreds of kilometers away, make the decision of what our food should be on property we would never even see. In addition, to be able to actually taste.

And see how our produce is treated to prevent conditions like diseases and illnesses and what the soil requires growing it. We automatically follow little-flavored cherries, no pigment except the thin red facade, merely because they are plentiful and affordable. Why are we carrying this on? We are doing so because we have missed the meaning of our Connection with one of our life's most important and essential aspects — our food.

4.1 Planning the Right Architectural Design

Residential landscaping can be described as the art and practice of enhancing the appearance and architectural appeal of a home environment. Every home and its landscape should be a representation of the people living there. This reflects the first experience a tourist gets of the home and its occupants. Once first noticed, the visitor will be quickly greeted and guided to the front door. The ecosystem will be usable, too. An appealingly landscaped home not only provides the family residing their satisfaction, it also enhances the community and significantly contributes to the house.

The aim of this chapter is not to be a model for landscape creation but rather a framework for preparing and making decisions along with an overview of the concepts involved in landscape design. Hence there is no need to feel scared about a residential landscaping scheme. The summary in this chapter will let you know exactly what to expect if you are redeveloping an established yard or landscaping for residential development. You should break down the service of landscaping your yard into two stages: design and implementation.

The design stage compromises of primary research, collection of information, and preparation. During this process, you, the homeowner, should work closely with a residential designer or architect who specializes in landscape design. Together you will discuss system design such as the particular goal for your yard, which amenities will be included, and which type of landscaping will be hired. The design phase finishes with you having a completed plan that recommends place and components for hardscapes and elements of living outdoors as well as plants. The phase of construction includes the actual construction process.

Many planners may apply the job to a residential landscaping contractor contracting company. Sometimes one firm will do all of the work; others will involve multiple firms. The planner and contractor must work closely together during this process to carry the design plan generated in the preceding phase to existence. Upon checking and washing, your yard will be turned into space at the end of the building, which is prepared for you to experience with friends and relatives.

Designing the Landscape

- Get ideas for the reason, functionality and design you like (internet, books, magazines)
- Fill in a questionnaire on architecture.
- Enable an expenditure

- Meet future designer / contractor
- Select a specialist
- Planning workshop and ground review
- Meeting of review
- Full acceptance of the program

When Starting the Landscaping Project

- Examine projections for building
- Demolition (if required) of unnecessary materials and structures;
- Grading (guarantees adequate water supply)
- Water park (excavated & built)
- Electrical conduits operate (water, coal, electricity)
- Enable a watering system
- Walls installed (rest, periphery, seating)
- Hardscapes are created (patio, floor, tracks)
- Build living external components (recreational kitchens, fireplaces, etc.)
- Seedling
- Checking (irrigation, coal, electric) networks
- Full washing and sweeping

Small Landscape Ideas for Your Residence

The smaller landscapes in the garden are extremely informative. There is no space for poor planning or incompleteness, whether the landscape graces a condominium, a small bungalow, or a rooftop. That is how what is ignored is gradually transforming into an ugly mess. Given their diminutive nature, small gardens may often have as diverse plant palettes as a larger area. Mini garden escapes will vary from cozy cottage designs to sleek, contemporary looks. Landscaping designs could also use smaller plant varieties, smaller plants, and other modified products to meet the constraints of space in a limited area. A smart planner does not scale down the same landscape layout used by a palatial estate but instead understands how to accentuate and represent a tiny outdoor space's daintier proportions. You should find advice from landscaping experts on:

- Three simple techniques in tight conditions, for good landscape architecture.
- How to generate many tiny points of reference in small garden open space that can come as surprises when discovered unexpectedly.
- Why it is necessary, when planning a small garden, to think in square inches rather than foot.

- The key distinctions between planning a greenhouse on the rooftop and planning a residential landscape.
- Plotting a rooftop garden challenge including mass, availability, air and leaf width, plant length.
- Suggestions for small landscape features that may fit many functions, like built-in storage bench seating.
- Your annuals, ferns options made to fit into selected ways.
- Herbaceous perennials flexible to odd-sized areas and small gardens.
- To avoid crowding overhangs and eaves, how to opt for dwarf shrubs for a small garden that matches the diameter of the expanding area and meet height limitations.
- Ideas about how to incorporate a single tiny tree as both a central focus and an issue solver in a small yard.
- Why it is essential to use a small garden with the finest materials you can afford.
- Where to incorporate various features of landscaping into a tiny backyard.
- How to plan a small yard to include a pool, a patio, a fire pit, and a lawn field.
- Suggestions for landscaping a wide side yard utilizing shade and retaining walls.

- Solutions to address traditional problems in the small-yard environment, such as anonymity, adequate ventilation, and noise, and wind blockage.
- How and when to incorporate paving components into the interior floor coverings used in a mini garden.
- Limited shade gardens with layout and seedling solutions.

Whenever it comes to small garden, design, it is essential to pay attention to the specifics, plan each inch, add surprises, and spend the cash on materials. Whether you are deciding to create a very potent and exciting little room or a contemporary utilitarian one, a skilled landscaper can help you bring your little garden to life.

Defining bounds

The house is set in or near the middle of the lot on many landfill sites, and the front lawn is an accessible, unverified lawn area. Most of the landscaping is situated right in front of the building and does not reach more than a few feet apart. This openness causes the house to lack unity with the rest of the lawn. Moreover, the lack of established boundaries or edges incorporates one front yard into the next, making the driveway as the only item which separates one property from the next.

An easy approach to combine the plantation with the lawn near to the house is to stretch the planting bed many feet out into the lawn. These beds move more comfortably from the corners of the room, but do not need to be limited to this. Expanding the planting or concreted area close to the entrance can be both visually effective and functional, as it allows a few people to arrive at the entrance comfortably. Extended beds may contain trees and shrubs, or they may consist entirely of ground cover; either of these may help link the house to the countryside.

Routes for Navigation

The position, distance, design, and choice of your path network products can affect how the landscape is used. The routes decide how the environment is being navigated, and show viewpoints and framing areas. Not all tracks have the same function: some, the primary routes, will outperform the view and determine the plan of the garden. Infrequently, the secondary roads are used to take you off the major thoroughfare to enter locations shielded from sight, for either functional or design purposes.

Main routes

The primary route or pathway through the landscape not only connects the various areas together but also defines the general architecture. For starters, the main path straight down the middle implies formality, while a curved path through the garden provides the basis for a casual design. A broad path provides an accessible, welcoming pathway that attracts tourists, and a small, twisting path that is flanked by tall planting that obscures the view adds intrigue. Use a focal point, such as a bench, statue, or container, to set a visual boundary to punctuate the end of the route. A primary route should be extensively utilized by its design, so products need to be both robust and conducive to the overall landscape theme. Consider how the form and composition of the edges of the path work into the pattern, too.

Secondary Sidewalks

While primary routes evaluate a garden's style, supplementary routes should be less invasive and subtly embedded in the design. They may be utilitarian as well as ornamental, offering intermittent exposure to a sitting room, barn, or compost heap, or taking you off the main track on an enjoyable journey to see a hidden corner.

They can also slash across large flowerbeds, enabling you to get a close experience with colors and scents. Access routes need not be as sturdy as main paths and can be formed through a grassy patch from lighter, organic materials or mown through.

Know, the landscape of your residence gives your friends and acquaintances their first view of you and your family. You will build a landscape with a clear curb appeal by adopting the principles described above: one that is coherent, sustainable, and coordinated with the property and the community and, at the very same time, a distinctive representation of you and your preferences.

4.2 Practical Considerations

Let us admit it; it is a struggle to include edible plants in landscape design and to make it really come out good. Sprinkling cabbage leaves, wild tomatoes, and scruffy peppers with bare seeds are the explanation that so many vegetable crops are confined at the farthest corner of the field – generally tucked away in only a few backyard beds.

With some simple shortcuts and suggestions, we are about to teach you how to do that in your own yard. We discover that graphic examples of design features are the quickest way to get ideas, so we have collected a range of potential vegetable patch features/resources that you can use. Whether you are thrifty, inventive, just searching for ease fast, you will find solutions to match your time and budget like DIY, free / upcycled and company choices.

Guidelines & Preparation - Creation of a Simple Edible Landscape

To plan your landscape, you do not need to be an artist or an expert at writing a landscaping blueprint. Many people create thorough to-scale drawings, and some only compose loose notes on a sheet of paper behind a scrap and then eyeball both until they get into the yard. Another smart approach to create an edible landscape design: consider a traditional landscape design and replace the plants in the design with edible plants.

Any drawing stationary + sheet of paper (or the unprinted side of last night's burger box) would do for this exercise when you are about to continue sketching!

However, when confronted with the potential for new office equipment at the start of a worded project, unless you are some kind of individual who has to limit himself or herself from rolling about like a cat in catnip, here are some beneficial garden design techniques that go beyond guilty pleasures:

- A journal for the "decomposition" of thoughts and drawings-a variation on a journal for the "composition."
- A modeling stencil device suitable for edible landscape creation
- Recycled Paint Sticks

Realistic Considerations for an Edible Design of the Landscape:

There is a realistic dimension of edible landscape architecture, besides the creative aspect of stuff. Below you may need to remember five important elements while preparing your edible landscape:

Microclimates

Know your yard's spots that get the greatest, and the least, sunshine. Using a compass or enter your address into suncalc.net (shade-casting items as if trees and buildings would need to be accounted for).

In summer, most vegetables and fruits take a number of 6 hours of sunshine per day to produce well. There are heaps of edible plants, however, which also grow flawlessly well in the shade.

Water Fountains

Where is your backyard water supply? In drought spells, there may be an irrigation device, spigot, hose, dam, rainwater floodplain, or another source of moisture. You can haul a bucket to the far reaches of the yard, of course, but it is easier to prepare ahead, so it does not have to happen — and that you are edible garden remains well maintained.

Soil Issues

Where in your backyard are the most issue soles? Too hot, dusty, rough, muddy, flat or filthy? Every position should be remembered. Try to solve these difficulties or place the garden somewhere else.

Note: Read more about Soil and Nutrients later in this chapter.

Ease of Access without Moving

Do not get through it! Part of having good soil and terrific garden design does never have to step into a bed for sorting, irrigating, harvesting, sowing, or whatever else.

It induces compaction of the soil and is harmful to the plants. All beds should be designed as single-range beds (about 2' wide and used against walls, fences, or other obstacles) or as a double-range bed (about 4' wide, or as long as your arm can reach from all sides to the center). Broad cultivated borders greater than 4' will have concealed pathways or stepping stones and use double or single-reach dimensions so, and you can navigate every inch of the landscape for upkeep without compacting the soil—you want to be sure that you can find and quickly utilize your defined walking areas so that you are not tempted to move in your bed "just this once."

Set of Plants

What plant types do you wish to grow? Most edible plants seek either a "meadow" setting (including most seed-grown annual vegetables) or a "hill" (often-woody shrubs and perennials on the understory). Remember because, after a tree falls, most forest plants are chancers who grow their best, and the ensuing canopy void allows them maximum sun for another few years. For safer crops and heavy growth, you should build your beds to match those preferences. For starters, use heavy wood chip mulches; you might place your "meadow" beds in direct sunlight with lightweight manures of straw and leaves, and your "forest" grounds in maximum to partial sunlight.

Topography

Have you ever observed a position in your lawn pooling in the downpour and seemingly always mushy? Alternatively, a location seemingly needing more moisture than just about anywhere else does. In addition, on a limited scale, topography plays a significant role in designing a landscape by dictating how precipitation passes across the soil. A decreased spot can mean that nearly all of the root system is lounging in the water.

Although water is healthy for the roots, far too much water is depriving the origins of oxygen and producing an uninhabitable atmosphere in the soil for beneficial bacteria. Most plants can fail without these and ultimately die. Repeatedly wet places may be especially suited to ornamental wetlands, while edibles are maintained to lawn areas that are stronger drained. There can also be some difficulties to a large, dry region since soil microbes can dry out rapidly.

This can usually be handled easier than a low wet environment, although it does require constant irrigation to avoid the drying out of roots. A dense mulch layer on a large, dry region of planting can aid delay movement of moisture and retain it longer in the soil. A dry area could be a good place for edibles that are somewhat drought resistant, like Mediterranean origin herbs: oregano, thyme, sage, rosemary.

82

Such edibles would need sufficient water to establish themselves, but they can manage warmer temperatures too. In a dry environment, too chard and mustard veggies would do well. However, for a sizeable chunk of plants to make things

4.3 Cultivating Your Own Plants

Through cultivating your own produce, endless benefits arrive, no matter where or how you do it. If you have ever developed any of your own fresh produce, you know the exuberance of increasing exciting, extraordinary cultivars and the accomplishment of having to bring your food to your table right from your yard. Of course, the taste is also a major part of the picture. There is something special about the taste of a tomato or sweet potato that you pulled out of your own plant right away. A beautiful happiness comes from the awareness that the hard work and caring made these plants develop into vibrant, bountiful plants from tiny seeds. Nothing will ever quite contrast to the distinct sweetness of a tomato crop picked from the vineyard with the warm sun persisting in the flavorings, nor the gentle chomp of another-picked bean or the perfect gentleness of green beans right out of the veggie patch. These aromas are what drives so many of us to spend many hours tending and pampering on our knees, smudging our toenails with soil—the promise of real sun tasting – sweet, rich, nutritional meals.

An effective landscape and lawn are all about equilibrium. A combination of trees, vegetables, crops, and herbs in your backyard is building a vibrant environment. Growing together, edibles and ornamentals deliver benefits that go beyond aesthetic appeal and fresh produce. The mere mingling of a large number of plants makes a garden safer, and thus easier to manage. You've learned how mono-cropping is harmful in large-scale agriculture, as planting just one seed contributes to a lack of resources, disease occurrence, and issues with insect pests, which ensures major losses if a crisis occurs. Planting too much of one crop ensures that once a pathogen or pest discovers one plant that it wants, it is forced to eat all the rest — and that's not good for yields. Hence, diversified agriculture is such a good idea. Getting a plant mix implies damage, and the nutrient requirements are shared over several different crops. Even if an insect bug hits one crop, the other crops are likely to be all right and compensate for the damage. While not depending entirely on one seed, chances of production are higher. There are heavy feeders like cucumbers when it comes to nutrients that take up many nutrients in the soil as they grow, and there are gracious dietary-providers like beans that actually give back to the soil. There is sun-worshipping squash that requires the brightest position in the lawn, and there are easy-going greens that take whatever bit of sun is left over. There are plague-sensitive plants that could be seriously damaged by pests or illnesses, and there are crops that help ward off insects or scare away pest enemies. A varied plantation also means there is a lot of pollinator food and other native species that are essential for any farm or garden. The more we can trap insects, the more of our crop. It is the equilibrium of this normal sharing and taking that is intrinsic in naturally existing habitats that we can strive in our gardens and landscapes to accomplish. This balance would be part of what makes it so rational, amusing, wonderful, and ultimately futile for this type of landscaping.

Plantation Structure

Often neglected, planting structure can be complicated for young and seasoned gardeners equally. Using the following tips to ensure that your garden's plantings serve a specific function and draw humans, bees, butterflies, and birds' interest.

Responsibly Pick Plants for the Front Line

The plants along a path, deck, or lawn at the noticeable edge will make a world of difference in its presentation. In the front row, low-growing plants accentuate bed shape, lighten harsh corners, and attract better interest to the harder and longer behind.

Limited-growing plants will be complete in the front row, look fine in a line, and should not take too much attention. When you look from a distance at a garden bed, the height of the edging plants will be fairly high — about 2 feet. The boundary plants will be less than 2 feet in beds, which are seen up close. Annuals like the sweet alyssum and its thick, small, aromatic white flowers make an excellent white edging. When cutting back, they bloom in the season. Some of my favorites for edging beds is the annual white and green varied lily turf (Liriope muscari)

Know the Color Impact of Natural Light

For the most part, our color preferences in the countryside are determined by our geographical position, the strength of the sun, and the time of year. In England, for example, pastel colors fascinate while bright colors in the subdued, north light may appear garish. That is why the popular British garden developer Gertrude Jekyll saw purple as a challenging color. However, every hue of purple and fuchsia is joyously enticing in a luminous, warm spring tropical orchard.

Likewise, our preferences for color can alter the transfer period. We are fascinated by bright pink and gentle yellow in the early morning, whenever the sun is warm.

When the year continues as the light becomes hotter, pastels appear washed out, and we are searching for more natural darks like reds, golds, and citrus.

Think About Type, Line & Hue

Plants are not often referred to as an arabesque, meaning a sinuous ornamental line or motif.

Captivation of Leaves, And Scent - Build a Tapestry Out Of It

Although we can grow a huge mass with one low-growing crop as just a ground cover, Nature tends to combine it with other species rising side by side, if given a preference. Why do not they do the same and grow a confluence of various plants of vegetation and ground cover that prefer the same environments? Some recommend against this planting method, as intertwined crops may be challenging to care for. Yet if you do not like a monolithic feel, and do not care over the tenderness, plant a mix of tiny-leaved ground coverings with huge-leaved plants. The outcome can be mesmerizing!

Include Nutrition for the Nose

The scent provides nourishment of the ears. A human takes 23,000 breaths per day on balance, and the fragrances in each breath convey knowledge, mood and evoke memories in a manner that nothing else can.

Here are tips for embedding perfumed crops in a landscape:

- Position aromatic plants in the area of your home, and you can catch a taste of the scent when you walk the house.
- Place fragrant plants on a bright deck, or next to a wall facing south. The heat reflected can make the scents slightly stronger.
- Grow fragrant trees, including a gated community or tiny side yard, inside an enclosed environment. Instead of being swept out by the wind, the smell will gather, so that you will be covered by perfume.

Pollinators Recall

A garden, we frequently look past, is an intricate nature of the world. As we enjoy the light, scent, and starlings, butterflies, constantly pollinate feel of a beautiful field, our plants flies, birds, and much more. Global research shows that several causes, particularly habitat loss, trigger pollinator species to decrease, so please try creating your backyard a sanctuary for these incredible creatures.

You will begin drawing pollinating insects to your backyard by growing nectar-rich bulbs, trees, and bushes — talk of the shades they like too. Hummingbirds, for example, are especially fond of red while bees appear to prefer purple / violet flowers.

In late summer, many plants make fruit or seed to drop when birds prepare to move south. The fruit of such plants as dogwood crabapple, dogwood (Cronus), and blueberry add interest to the scenery while feeding our fellow creatures.

In addition, you may even suggest growing one of the several varieties of Viburnum. In the fall, Viburnum berries draw a variety of birds, namely robins, songbirds, catbirds, thrushes, cardinals, sparrows, and waxwings.

Uncover more shrubs and fruit-bearing trees. Chokeberry (Aronia arbutifolia) is a natural berried vine.

Which retains its red fruit during the winter. True to its name, this wetland shrub has very bitter fruits. Due to this, birds do not eat them until they have undergone several cycles of thaw/freeze. Thus, the berries do provide color and winter food. The hardy, self-fertile 'Wiking' black chokeberry (Aronia melanocarpa 'Viking') is a chokeberry to seek. The huge berries and fruits last through the season, allowing the first robins to arrive.

Existing Plants

It is likely that you are not beginning your landscape with a completely empty or free backyard and already but have some Plants, bushes, and trees, and bushes living there. Such methods are useful in preparing your landscape by giving you hooks on which to work. At the front of the yard, you might have possibly the best-placed trees or shrubs that surround the property, or a beautiful lilac or hibiscus you do not want to split with. In addition, you certainly should not. Such existing plants grant a point of departure and make it easier to choose other plants than if you started with a nearly empty yard.

Getting Sunlight

Most plants that produce food favor six or more hours of sun per day. For eight hours or more, heat-lovers like peppers and tomatoes fare fine. This may be challenging to get across on a suburban street with tons of huge old trees. If this seems like your backyard and you are planning to develop any foodstuffs, you might need to be careful about where you choose to do this in your yard. Unless you already have some thriving garden beds and get plenty of sun, then operate there in some edibles.

Nevertheless, keep a few of those ornamentals for uniqueness. If you have no flower beds yet, take a good long look at your lawn at various times of the day and keep a record about where the light moves and the length of time each region is in the sun. This is among the most significant elements toward creating any type of productive garden or landscape.

You have to learn how light passes through your yard, how often shadow the ancient spruce sheds at the intersection, and where the shade shifts during the day. If not, your plant species will find it difficult, and you will probably spend years making up for it with crops and other stuff that will not happen. Plants require luminosity.

They need sunlight to generate the energy that they need to rise. Items like tomatoes should have a lot of light because creating large, juicy, flavorful fruits requires a lot of energy. Not only is the amount of light significant, or the length, but so is the value and wavelength of light. Any particular region that gets 6 hours of morning sun would be different from a place that gets 6 hours of afternoon sunlight.

Both are called full light, although, for certain plants, the afternoon sun is cooler than the morning sun, which may be a little too warm.

Plant a few heat-lovers such as okra, collard greens, Malabar broccoli, sweet peppers, and cucumber in an afternoon-sun location. Tomatoes, zucchini, beans, broccoli, and eggplant are planted in the morning-un fields.

Importance of Soil

The soil is the place where the alchemy takes place. Soil is composed of fragments of rocks, organic material, soil, water, and life. A combination of these various factors renders the soil optimal, but that is rare, particularly in industrial environments where compaction, pollution, and decades of usage are possible.

There might be soft sandy soil in your yard, hard clay soil, or anything in between. Soil texture extremes face problems for landscapers. Clay soil is tough as it is hard to dig in and split up, which drain very gradually.

A large percentage of sand produces a rather dry, thin soil, which can be difficult because sandy soil appears to drain very easily and does not give plant roots strong structure. Loam soil is a particle size medium, which is usually the safest for planting. However, most gardeners are not endowed with ideal loam soil in their yards and must modify it to make the land habitable to plants. Over time, this is generally done and is better accomplished by incorporating organic matter to the soil.

Organic matter and soil microorganisms ultimately decide how the soil holds together.

Organic material consists of anything that used to be awake: plants, animals, microorganisms that are all in numerous stages of decomposition. Millions of unknown microbes, alongside numerous species like insects and worms, function synergistically to disintegrate the soil organic matter, and then leads to soil composition, air and water transport, and nutrient recovery.

Organic matter is essential to green, stable plants in the soil. The more organic matter in the ground, the further bacteria are involved.

The further involved the bacteria, the more nutrition they produce for crops, and the healthier the condition of the soil. The higher the soil composition, the simpler it is to travel across air and water and to grow plant roots. Organic matter increases the capability of the soil to receive, hold, and transfer water. It works like a sponge, able to attract water and soak it up, converting it throughout the soil to other sponge-like particles of organic matter.

Nutrients in the Soil

Humans need good nutrients, and plants do so. Most landscapers are acquainted with plants needing major nutrients (macronutrients) — nitrogen, phosphorus, and potassium — since they're the basic nutrients in most commonly available fertilizers: N-P-K; There are also other nutrients plants need to grow actively and to be successful in smaller quantities, recognized as micronutrients. Thanks to organic matter, many of these are generally present in the soil. Yet some of those nutrients are likely to be exhausted after successive years of massive plants in the soil. Even though annual vegetables sprout so rapidly and take up much more amounts of nutrients, regions of the garden that are primarily planted with these can quickly become depleted.

That is one reason why it is such a good idea to combine many flowering varieties — various plants utilize nutrients at various speeds, and many even offer additional nutrients to the soil. When soil nutrients are out of balance, crazy things happen in the garden: leaves change color, brown, or other unusual colors; leaves are misshapen; plant species feel wilted given with plenty water; plants seem to stop developing; strawberries, tomatoes, and other berries are oddly shaped. Which are mostly the product of nutritional deficits, but excess nutrients may also pose certain problems.

Chances are you can go a fair way to providing and sustaining a healthy climate for your plants by planting a broad range of herbs and ornamentals, perennials and annuals, shrubs, and trees. You are guaranteed to provide a balanced, productive, bountiful, and magnificent ecosystem through frequent applications of manure, cover-cropping, mixed cropping, and the periodic addition of nutritionally boosting chemical manure.

Discovering Options of Plants

If you first start browsing at seed catalogs or make lists of the plants you want to use in your edible landscape, it may seem a little daunting. So many options can be difficult. Take tomatoes, for instance. You have the heirlooms that pose a vast array of choices right there.

So fascinating are the strange forms and colors, not to mention the variety of flavors. Apply to this the synthetic types and massively growing the possibilities. Specify, infinite, strawberry, orange, beefsteak, early season, late season. How do you decide?

The initial thing you should do is sit down and draw up a list. Include every fruit and vegetable you enjoy eating on that list. Unless you are like me, the file is going to be very large. Even if you believe, the plant may be difficult to grow, or may not grow in your climate, add it to the list. There may be an option to build a non-hardy plant in a container, or a similar plant could be used as an alternative. Write down what you think. There is scope for the subsequent recording.

Tomatoes, onions, beans, cucumbers, and basil would be on top of other lists. These garden staples are popular because they are relatively simple to develop; they quickly start from seed, yield a lot during the season, and are delicious fresh from the field. Let your imagination stretch a little now. Dream of heading to the grocery store or market for the growers. What are the foods that catch your eye when they are in a season that you can never pass up? Sparrows? Cherries Pie? Springs up in Brussels? Apples? Potatoes, right?

Everything to write down. Page through a seed catalog or peruse one online, if you need a little inspiration. You may undoubtedly be told of a few things you enjoy, enjoy artichokes, okra, or cranberries that you might never have dreamed about developing yourself. In your yard, matching plants to the light is a reasonably straightforward way to make some initial choices. Know, to be robust and efficient.

Most food-producing plants require six to eight hours of maximum sunlight.

You will optimize the sunny areas by choosing the right plants for the right spot, and still allow the use of the less bright areas.

Sunlight and Plants

If you have just a little full sun in your yard, save that area for the sun-lovers, it is the place for some tomatoes in heaven. Nestle in any lettuce, onions, and eggplant alongside the tomatoes. The achillea (yarrow) is one of my favorite perennials for a pop of color in sunny regions. While it is not nutritious, it is bright, quick to develop and split, and will draw countless beneficial insects. Signet marigold, a small-flowered, mounding marigold, is an ideal option for planting around the tomato base, mostly because it provides a vibrant foundation for those big, green plants. Petunias or other annual trailing works well also around the base of taller plants. They fill the understory with color and may even help by filling in the space under tall plants to keep weeds away. Okra is another excellent choice for sunny surroundings. Okra is commonly thought to be a plant in the South, but that is not true. If started indoors in the early spring and in the northern landscape, okra can be a beautiful plant.

Its hibiscus-like creamy white or yellow flowers give way to striking, edible pods in colors from light green to deep burgundy. A beautiful and unusual plant adds considerable interest to the landscape. Other sunny spot favorites include squash, cucumbers, strawberries, herbs, and melons. Strawberries can handle a little less sun, but a brilliant sunny spot will grow bigger, healthier, and more flavored. Interpolated with bright, sun-loving annuals and perennials, all of these plants will make your yard's sunny places colorful, lush, and above all delicious!

Easy Partial-Sun Plants

Luckily, there are quite a few plants that do not have to worship the sun just as much as the tomato, which is more than happy to relax now and then in a bit of shade. Such plants are the backbone of every edible landscape, providing color, texture, and beauty in an undemanding natural climate. Greens make up most of this group, and of the greens, chard is one of the best in the kitchen for its range of colors, ease of growth, and many uses. Kale and other greens are beautiful additions to the landscape's less-sunny areas and perfect in the oven. The various kale varieties include your garden with a range of color and fascinating leaf shapes and textures.

The leaves range in color from blue-green to purple-red, all with a silver-gray tinge that makes them an excellent backdrop for annuals and perennials that are brightly colored. In addition, Kale is very nutritious and can be used in salads, soups, sautés, etc.

Lettuces, mustard greens, arugula, and all kinds of baby greens add colorful sparks to the landscape throughout the season, especially if they are kept out of full sun's heat. All the lettuces and small greens are fun to use as border plants. They can be a tremendous edible alternative to annual ornamental bedding plants thanks to the different colors and leaf texture available.

4.4 Creative Ideas for Further Recreation

Everybody wants to see their patio or lawn look their highest quality without spending loads of money, doing a major revamp of the existing layout, or repairing what isn't broken — and that is understandable. That is why here is a collection of the very best suggestions for your landscape out there. Below are some fantastic ideas, creative tips, and wise solutions for both your children and lawn that you can execute on a budget easily and conveniently.

Flower ramparts

If you have an exterior tub, with a floral curtain, build a perfect sense of anonymity. Throughout this backyard, growing shrubs like hydrangeas by the landscape expert Ed Hollander (or flowers that do not bother dampness) will operate like a breathing shower curtain (and appear to be better value for money), while they boost the smell of intimacy in a romantic environment already. Assure the trees are pruned, so moist sunshine will flood in.

Rooftop meals

Take notice of a Venice Beach loft if you stay in a busy community with the limited open area but have connections to the rooftop. A wooden covering produces a lovely speckled light impression, and crafted pendants offer the vibes of space holidays.

Outdoor Douche

Lay a tile route that leads the way to make a remarkable open-air shower look even more glorious. Then hang up wall art on the outside wall so you can show off your beautiful towels. They are a perfect way to put in a range of shades, without growing a whole yard.

Lanterns in the Wood

Give some attention to your plants, and spice up the yard by placing lanterns in the limbs. That will set the tone for a truly beautiful living space outdoors.

Luminous design

The beauty of creative lighting installation is that at night you can design a completely different look for your garden. Sweet, elegant illumination is simple and allows the most of various materials and contours, putting only a few preference features into view. Given the wide variety of advanced lighting equipment available, a more dramatic style is feasible. These are essential health and protection issues to remember, and you can speak to an electrician regarding your plans.

Beaming In the Garden

Flooding the garden with light from above produces an impact that is too harsh and can cause neighboring disturbance and contribute to the light pollution issue. Stop bright lights that will glare right through an onlooker 's eyes. Through having shadow areas, you can accentuate the dramatic impact of every garden setting and render the nighttime atmosphere much more enchanting.

Draw up design, taking into account the form of lighting needed in-region, such as recessed illumination for a deck.

Or underwater lighting for a well. Function transformer or find it inside a building in a waterproof container.

A transformer reduces the voltage from the highs to a lower stage where other devices for garden lighting operate. The size of the transformer you'll need depends on how efficient and how many lights you want to use. Tell the electrician to mount cable cables and connection points indoors and speak to a professional electrician or lighting specialist about the suggestions, hopefully before you finish some new landscaping projects. By simply using a strong torch or torches, kept at various angles, you will play with different lighting results.

Small twinkle LED lights running from a transformer are simple to mount and build a romantic mood when placed on a pergola by climbers. Mini spots are perfect for illuminating an architectural plant or a statuary object or for highlighting textured surfaces. Low-level recessed lighting in stages, walls, and decks shed soft illumination without glare, and colored lighting may be used to produce contemporary effects, floodlights, or make walls or water pools. Seek tiny white or colorful LED spots built into a decked area or a few underwater lights to light up a transparent, reflective pool for a contemporary feel.

Water Features

Like no other garden element, water fascinates and captivates. Its movement, reflections, and sound give a garden an appealing mix of new sensations. Water also provides the ability to cultivate a number of plants that will draw butterflies and other animals to the greenhouse, whether you are growing a natural pond or supplementing a conventional building.

Small elements such as spouting figures and heads or an overflowing urn may be put in borders between the planting for a natural look. Ponds do best in good light, away from trees and falling leaves, rotting and polluting the water. Place them even away from utility channels, such as power cables. Both equipment should be used as an important part of the architecture and positioned where trees, rocks, or decking may conceal some filters and pumps. The health of children is a key concern too.

Conclusion

If you've never done landscaping before, it can be daunting to start with, particularly when you're thinking of all the decisions you have to choose. But, it is also an artistic adventure full of surprises to choose from hundreds of plant species and to recognize countless numbers of landscape features. Your layout will always start with a concept, from a small front lawn to a vast landscape. Think of the income, competencies, yard scale, area, and upkeep while planning a do-it-yourself venture. Link to the environment while creating a design by holding plants in balance and size in check.

But, as mentioned earlier in this book, the same principles that guide the setup of your room can also guide your designs outside. So do not worry, below are some tips that will basically summarize the entire book for you. So, If you want to employ a skilled landscape designer, formulate a plot map of your land, including your backyard or front yard is among the first items he/she will do. That is obviously something you can handle yourself.

- Draw a bird's-eye view of your house, noticing all the human-made elements (called hardscape), including houses, barriers, driveways, stone walls, etc. Pebbles, trees, and broad shrubs unite to create the "core" of your landscape with your hardscape.

- Using graph paper facilitates, so you don't have to be agonizing over precise proportions, a more proportional drawing would be perfect.
- Make sure your well, septic scheme, or any submerged utility lines are included. Direct a bunch on the map and see where the dark, bright places are.

Once you recognize something you already have, you can proceed to prepare a note of what you would like to possess. How would you like the appearance of your garden? Begin with a couple of general targets. For instance:

- Would you like a patio area of privacy?
- Do you want to screen an annoying view?
- Is your primary concern curb appeal / auction-value or a more discreet view?

However, it can also be possible that your hardest dilemma regarding landscaping is to decide what and how to plant. The wisest guidance that we might give you? Choose the perennials, the crops that return to existence each year. Similarly, select young crops, trees and shrubs, and also plant species indigenous to your area. So, you invest the lowest amount of cash and have the finest chance to keep it healthy and never have to substitute it. Yes, if you unexpectedly have the urge to do more landscape design once you've tackled such simple landscaping tasks (and we expect you do so), you may also take parts of your current perennials and grow them somewhere else in subsequent seasons. Armed with a practical and very well-thought-out landscaping strategy, over many years you will spread the effort and cost. To prevent the idea from being stressful taking things one move at a time. Remember that should be fun! You create a space where you can enjoy yourself. Over the years, slow, incremental changes will turn your backyard into the heaven you dream.

References

1. The Benefits of Landscapes. Retrieved from: https://www.loveyourlandscape.org/benefits/the-benefits-of-landscapes/

2. Landscape Design Principles for Residential Gardens. Retrieved from: https://www.gardendesign.com/landscape-design/rules.html

3. Planting Ideas for Your Garden. Retrieved from: https://www.gardendesign.com/ideas/planting.html

4. Landscape Maintenance Checklist. Retrieved from: https://www.homeadvisor.com/r/landscape-maintenance-checklist/

5. Outdoor Fountain Ideas. Retrieved from: https://www.landscapingnetwork.com/fountains/

6. Types of Landscape Design. Retrieved from: https://guzmansgreenhouse.com/types-of-landscape-design/

7. Beginner Landscaping. Retrieved from: https://www.tdp-arch.com/news-updates/landscaping-for-beginners

8. Landscaping Ideas for Low-Maintenance Yard. Retrieved from: https://www.popularmechanics.com/home/lawn-

garden/how-to/g2581/landscaping-ideas-for-low-maintenance-yard/

9. Residential Landscaping. Retrieved from: https://extension2.missouri.edu/mg11

10. Different Landscaping Tools and Their Uses. Retrieved from: https://landscapeinnovations.org/different-landscaping-tools-and-their-uses/

.